MW00937446

LOVE NEVER DIES

∞

ELIZABETH HORWIN

Copyright © 2012 Elizabeth Horwin

All rights reserved.

ISBN: 148014388X

ISBN 13: 9781480143883

Library of Congress Control Number: 2012919941

CreateSpace Independent Publishing Platform

North Charleston, South Carolina

Dedication

This Book is Dedicated To
Michael, my Son, who taught me to Love
Unconditionally
And
Gary, my Husband, how together we taught each other
to accept Unconditional Love

ACKNOWLEDGEMENTS

I would like to acknowledge the enormous help given to me in the creation and unfolding of this book. For their patience, guidance and support, I wish to thank my friends, especially my network of girlfriends, who made this possible.

I would like to pay tribute to the many people who gave freely of their time and hearts to listen, to inspire and to encourage me during this four year process. A partial list of family and friends include my Mom, Elaine, Dorothy, Arlene, Doreen, Trudi, Lisa, Marie, Judy, Barbara, Cliessa, Liz, Valerie, Kim, Bobby, Beth, Tina, Susan, Jackie, Top, Tom, Paul, Dave, Bob, John and Joe.

Special thanks to Wendy, Mary, Ella, Karen, Lynn, Phyllis and Nathan who were willing to share their memories and experiences in print.

My profound gratitude to: Doctors Liam and Judd who directed me to the perfect publisher; Marilyn Derstine, my very patient and incredible editor; Lynn Tighe, Lori Scott, Nan Brenzel, my very dear friends who were there night and day encouraging me through every revision; and, Karen Bieryla McCarraher (my dear cousin who is more like my sister) supporting and loving me unconditionally through this process and through all of my experiences in this lifetime.

Finally and most importantly I want to express my deepest gratitude to my clients, my patients, who allowed me to assist them in navigating through their stages of loss and their healing process. I know you think you learned from me, but know that more often than not, it was I who learned from you. Thank you.

CONTENTS

PART ONE | page 1
What is Life?

PART TWO | page 23
What is Death?

PART THREE | page 49
What Do We Need to Understand?

PART FOUR | page 67
What Can We Do?

FOREWORD

Why do we fear death? Why do some people not fear death? Where do we go after we die? Is it the end of everything? Will we ever see our loved ones again? Is it death or the dying process we fear most? Is there really a God, Universal Intelligence, Source? Is what Teilhard de Chardin said true, "We are Spiritual Beings having a Human Experience"?

Love Never Dies examines and addresses all of these questions by focusing on the fundamental questions of life: who am I; where did I come from; why am I here; what is my purpose? Every time Spirit reincarnates to Earth, these questions must be addressed as Earth School is the training ground for Spirit/Soul Progression.

Love Never Dies will assist the reader, the teacher, the clinician, the student in examining these questions, these beliefs and then releasing fears associated with the concept of loss, death, dying and the dying process. It will help them come to the realization that the cycle of life in this earthly incarnation begins with birth of the physical body and ends with the death of the physical body. It is not life and death, but birth and death. The **Life of the Spirit** is **Eternal** and **Infinite**. It teaches the individual how to: understand and live through the stages of loss; understand relationships for what they are; become unattached to form and material possessions; implement a blueprint for not creating karma; appreciate the beauty of this planet and the divine plan; and trust in an orderly universe.

Love Never Dies was written with total respect for all religions, cultures and personal beliefs that have had their place in the progression of mankind. It is my hope that the insights provided regarding birth and death, energy and frequencies, cycles of life and the immortality of Spirit that comes from Source, God, and returns to Source will assist the reader in raising consciousness and awareness to the shift that is taking place on the Earth.

INTRODUCTION

SERVICE AND LOVE – THE ESSENCE OF LIFE

This morning I woke up before the new day was born. In the silence everything, all life, was at peace and still. Slowly as the light of day began to manifest, the stillness began to come to life. The energy and vibration of nature started to become enhanced as the darkness turned to light. A new day in the cycle of our planet—totally predictable, totally on time with no effort from us. The birds began their morning song, the geese rose to the sky as planet earth came to life, to purpose, to participate in the cycle of activity, growth and awareness until the evening returns and goes to night again before coming back to light.

This is more than a metaphor. This is an understanding of the flow, the cycles of life, the energy, the Spirit that vibrates in the form of our body as it participates effortlessly from one life to the next to the next.

Be not afraid, be glad. There is no such thing as death. There is birth, flow, peace and awakening. It is not Birth and Death; it is Birth and Continuous Life. It is the ebbs and flows of the cycle of life in each and every form at all times. It is the knowing that all remains in perfect harmony with the Source from which we came and to which we return.

As humans come to the realization of a shift of consciousness, that requires re-examining all beliefs based on fear, control, envy, greed, jealousy and all the emotions, values, beliefs that resonate with a lower frequency. The question of what is life's purpose then becomes the true understanding of why we are here—to reincarnate to learn, to balance, to love, to return to the Source from which we came, the Source that we are.

The answer is personal responsibility for all that happens in our life, each moment, each day, each decision. Imagine if the collective consciousness of the planet knew and lived this. There would be no need for rules, laws and dogmas. The human race in general is far from that level of consciousness, but on the planet today there are those that are quite conscious. In the evolution of this planet there were great teachers that paved the way like Abraham, Buddha, Jesus and Mohammed.

Focus on what matters, and what is that? It is Peace, Contentment, At-One-Ment with All. Focus on what matters. What we focus on increases; what we resist persists. Conflict, competition, striving and stressing defer our focus from the real purpose of life. It is quite obvious that the goals set up by unenlightened people aren't working. Violating universal laws, greed, hatred, fear (mostly fear) diminishes our ability to focus on what is really real and on purpose. Our purpose is to **Love** and **Serve**.

Love Never Dies, but one does **Die** without **Love**. The **Source** of all **Love** is **God**. I choose to call God Universal Intelligence that lives in me as Innate Intelligence. You call it whatever you want, whatever is comfortable for you. This is what I am sure of, am certain of, Love manifests itself in Service and this Service is to Humans and all Living Things. It's our job in this human experience to figure out how to Serve, how to Love Unconditionally without Judgment, Attachment or Resistance to the Flow of Life.

PART ONE

∞

WHAT IS LIFE?

Cycles of Day & Night
Flow of Life
Intervals of Life
Life is Energy
Frequencies: Life to Life

Cycles of Day & Night

The tree at the break of day stands in silence undisturbed in its awakening to the birth of a new day. It passed through the darkness of the night to stand firm and solid with the new day. Is this not true, symbolic and significant for our understanding of life? The cycles of day and night are the microcosm of the macrocosm of birth and death that can assist us in our understanding of Spirit, of Source.

The cycles of the day with total precision turn to night and night to day in perfect order every day. The ebbs and tides are the micro and we are the macro, our lives, and the Spirit in us that flows in perfect harmony. **ALL LIFE IS ENERGY.** The experience Spirit is having exists in the rhythm in every kingdom, be it the mineral, the plant, the animal or the human kingdom. In the time before day-light—the soft gray of the sky—the earth begins to awaken. If you are awake at this time and are silent, you could feel life coming to life—the birds, the wind or life's silence. Darkness brings Light. Stillness makes way for Activity. And so it is with the Ebbs and Flows of your Life. You cannot have the Light without the Darkness; you cannot have the Positive without the Negative, and the Joyous without the Painful Experiences. Once you are Aware of this, once you get it, the labeling of Good or Bad, Happiness or Sadness, Health or Sickness goes away because you know that in form the experience was your choice designed with the assistance of your guides prior to incarnating into this life. This awareness leads to knowing, to Source, to God without the barriers, walls, dogma or fear.

FLOW OF LIFE

Why the highs and lows, why the pain and joy....well, it is part of the cycle....but then again, why....well, in order to feel the highs of love, the passion, the joys of life, you need to experience the lows.....but, why.....you'll never fully answer that question with the limitation we live with in the confines of mental, intellectual and rational thought. To Try Reduces the Magnificence of Infinity. Give up trying to answer the whys. The whys we should be asking if we are to progress in our spiritual and personal growth are about the beliefs we have been conditioned to accept, rather than searching for truth, for purpose, for why I am here.

The earth is so populated these days because so many Spirits—life source—have decided, chosen to come to Earth to experience the magnificence of the Earth shifting and evolving to a new level of Awareness and Consciousness. So many Spirits—life source—choose to incarnate because of the fabulous opportunities to serve, to balance karma, to learn and experience on earth today. Observing the cycles of days and nights, starting with awakening in the morning, your awareness will increase and with awareness a rise in your consciousness. It is our job to become aware and one with this Consciousness of Life.

INTERVALS OF LIFE

So it is with the intervals of life, one each time for each incarnation. The tree starts from the seed to grow to the large oak to eventually die. The life of a tree is no different than the life of a human, an animal, a flower, a fruit. It has its purpose, its presence for a cycle of birth to death in the awareness that our minds, limited as they are, perceives.......but, we know there is no such thing as death, just a return to Source.

If we were to just pay attention to the cycles of nature, observe breath, feel the ebb and flow of life.....FEAR dissipates in knowing. Once you know, you cannot not know. The biggest mistake one makes is putting structure and form into the flow of life...thinking, especially in the western world, that somehow in doing so we can control our destiny. This is as impossible as trying to stop a wave as it is ready to meet the shore. Have you ever seen anyone stop a wave by thinking and trying to define it by form and structure? Because we are so identified with form, we miss the beauty of the flow of life. It then saddens us when death occurs because we see it as losing, we say we are sorry; we mourn and sometimes never get past the mourning. **Attachment to Form Causes Sadness.**

We can get past the sadness. For a moment, be still—close your eyes and breathe. Imagine in your mind's eye someone whom you have loved that has passed to the next kingdom, plane of vibration, of life. Go into that space for a moment and feel—feel the Peace, feel the Love. If you can't, just keep trying periodically and you will, but you will need to accept your loss and be willing to give up the need to be a victim, to solicit sympathy, to give up the drama and most importantly, the fear of the unknown, of judgment.

For nearly fifty years I have been asking these fundamental questions of life since that day in high school when my girlfriend and her little sister were killed in an accident as their car was hit by a train. It changed my world as I know death has changed yours. Our loved ones do not die and we can communicate with them, we can communicate with the Spirit world of God. Almost everyone that I have ever spoken to questioning their communication with loved ones that have passed acknowledges that they have had an experience, a feeling, a dream—something that assured them their loved one lives. What I have learned is that those who haven't had these experiences are usually stuck in one of the stages of loss, of mourning, or don't know how to begin the healing process. Later in this manuscript we will address these issues.

LIFE IS ENERGY

All life vibrates on frequencies of crystal clarity to density. Let us look at the kingdoms, beginning with the mineral kingdom. This kingdom contains the density of coal to the brilliance of diamonds. Energy exists and vibrates in each formation and so we have the spectrum from one end of the continuum to the next. Let us look at the vegetative kingdom from the weed to the orchid. It is the same spectrum. When we move to the animal kingdom-again, the pattern of vibrating energy is the same from the lowest level of insect to the dolphin. Now, in the human kingdom the same continuum of vibration and energy existing in the body of a mentally challenged, physically or emotionally challenged person to the brilliance of an Einstein or the love of Mother Teresa. Would it not follow that after the human kingdom the same continuum exists in the next kingdom, the Spirit kingdom? One might say, that's all we know for now, but is it? Do we not have glimpses into the Spirit world of

God—universal wisdom? God is in all kingdoms. We know the Spirit kingdom exists because we communicate with it and feel it...be it the protection of angels, the feeling of communicating with the saints, the presence energetically and sometimes physically of those we love that have passed. Does it make any sense that the vibration, energy and life stops after the human kingdom? Why would we consider that that is where life.....Source...stops and abides for eternity in a heaven or hell state. That defies logic and even those believers feel something doesn't make sense to believe in a notion of heaven and hell. There are more kingdoms to which our energy ascends; we just can't know them at our current level of consciousness.

As we continue to focus on form, let us look at all manifestations of form beginning with the mineral kingdom. Can we judge the good or evil of any form by placing a value on it based on our perception of its worth? Coal, it is black and dirty or so we say, but has it not provided heat, warmth, fuel to make our human life experience easier? A diamond is beautiful and impeccable. I ask, what purpose does it serve? What is its value? The answer is beauty. Is that value any greater than the warmth coal provides?

There is no predestination, but choice. How many lives does the Spirit, the energy that has taken human form want to experience? Does the form want a relaxation incarnation after many intense and difficult incarnations? Does the form want to balance three or four previous incarnations? Does it want to be in form with Spirit and energies from past lives to serve, to balance? Now, here is the thing. In each life amnesia sets in at birth, though children so close to the Spirit plane stay connected in that stream of consciousness. One can see it in their eyes. Now freewill comes in because you participated in the design of your life and the events unfold…..you choose your Response and that Response will determine Karma. For example, in deep hypnosis, in meditation, you get glimpses that resonate with you….deja vu….I've been here before…I am drawn here….I resonate with this…..why?

FREQUENCIES: LIFE TO LIFE

Can we really know and distinguish between the Spirit speaking and the form speaking? Yes, by paying attention. Our Spirit is Love and comes from the Source of all Love. When we are feeling the higher frequencies of Love and Compassion as we are Responding to life events, we know Spirit is speaking.

All nature, kingdoms, vitalistic beings are subject to the laws of frequency. Only humans on this plane are conscious of this. If that consciousness was ever present, the individual would choose the level of frequency moment by moment and would want to resonate with the higher frequencies of love, kindness, compassion, generosity and service. The choice would be obvious, but one cannot choose consciously if the awareness is not there.

The Aquarian Age is Water—fluid and clear. The density of mind is dissipating. What we have here is the shift from the Piscean Age—the warring for two millennia of good and evil, positive and negative. This duality comes together as one and the same—a continuum. The rise in awareness and consciousness is to the Now—to live in the Now, not the past or future, but the Now because that's all there is. The very concept of time and space dissolves. We need the concept of time and space to make sense of why our energy, our bodies are here. With the awareness that we are all one, that we all come from our Source to experience this life, to learn, to love, to balance karma and to enjoy the pleasures that earthly life offers, everything changes.

In awe we look at the night sky and see countless stars knowing that we are on this tiny planet in a solar system—one that we know of, not the countless others unknown to us. "Why am I here and what can I contribute?" This, in my opinion, should be the question of all humans, especially those of us who choose to live in a country, these United States, where for the first time in the history of this planet we are free to express the life force that we are—what we believe without fear of torture and death. Unfortunately the ideology of some groups of people is still subject to prejudice and condemnation even here in the United States, but this is changing.

We know how insane the world is, but there is hope if each and every one of us decides that we can be a light, a candle, in the darkness. We can only change ourselves, our perceptions. To start, all we need to do is be honest with ourselves about how we feel. We will feel good if we resonate with the higher frequencies of love, compassion, generosity and kindness and we will feel bad if we resonate with the lower frequencies of fear, jealousy, envy, hate, etc. It is our choice and by that choice we can change our world and the world.

If we realized how much we are loved, there would no isolation, no aloneness, and no fear. Universal Intelligence is Love and that Love exists in each and every one of us. Do we all manifest that love? Of course not if we are vibrating at the frequencies of jealousy, hate, envy, competition, control, etc., the lower frequencies.

Though Earth can be a lovely place to experience, it isn't an easy one except for maybe those enjoying a recreation incarnation. Because we come to Earth to learn, experience, serve and balance karma, it could be quite confusing, especially when those we love leave us, betray us or cause us to suffer because of our lack of understanding. We need to become aware and know that no one can cause us to suffer unless we allow them to.

For years before my Mom died when we'd discuss what happens after we die and will we see our loved ones again, I would tell her that there are more people on the other side that I like and am looking forward to being with than I have here now on Earth. We would laugh about that, but as everyone that Mom loved (she was the last of that generation) passed, we discussed that concept more in depth, even ideas that didn't fit the construct of her Roman Catholic belief system. Mom knew I had no fear of death and I would tell her about the white light and how those she loved would be waiting for her.

During Mom's final days in hospice, she didn't want to be in the facility where family and friends had died so hospice transported her to my sister's home where during her last ten days on this planet she had a room, privacy and could see nature through the window. We had a monitor in Mom's room and in the living room. One night shortly before Mom passed, I was staying overnight and reading in the living room when I heard voices. I couldn't quite understand what they were saying, but the voices were my Mom (Helen) and Cioci (aunt in Polish) Rosie, her older sister who had died ten years earlier. The conversation was muted (as it should have been) but some words were clear, like "Helen" and "Rose", and their voices were unmistakable. When they were done, I checked in on Mom and she was peacefully sleeping. The next morning when I walked into her room, we just smiled—she smiled the most radiant smile and she knew that I knew. Shortly after that experience, Mom needed to see and talk with only one other person, and then she went Home to join her loved ones.

I will end this section with another example of how we are assisted on our journey Home. My friend Ella shared this with me and allowed me to share it with you.

"As my sister was in her final days of a lengthy illness, she was where she wanted to be — at home. Her husband, sons, and I cared for her with hospice and other family and friends stopping in to check on her, too. The night before she left physicality, I had a sense that the time of passing was near, and I asked to stay overnight. I slept on the floor at the foot of her bed. In the morning, in that time just between sleep and wakefulness, I saw — in my mind's eye — a being lying on the bed beside her. Soon after that, I was fully awake, and her husband and I were attending to her. Within 30 minutes of the experience of someone there with her, she passed. It gave me comfort to know that my sister did not make the crossing alone."

PART TWO

∞

WHAT IS DEATH?

DYING
FEAR OF DEATH
RELATIONSHIPS CHANGE
RELATIONSHIPS ASSIST
RELATIONSHIPS CONTINUE

DYING

To accept anything, understanding is the first step. In essence, our consciousness needs to understand that it is Spirit and the form that Spirit takes changes from lifetime to lifetime. Spirit chooses to explore, learn, experience, serve and balance karma through form which is our body. That is how it works.

Taking someone's death personally causes unnecessary suffering. It is hard enough adjusting to the loss of the person's physical presence; why create more suffering by thinking that we have control over the death of anyone? We each have our sacred path and purpose for coming to planet earth. My job is to figure out my path and purpose, not to try and figure out what someone else chose.

Sometimes if we are willing to live through the mourning process and heal, we will get a glimpse of perhaps one of the reasons why someone died. In my experience this is usually a service. It took years after my son died before I realized that Michael's life with me and his death were both his service to me. Our relationship was one of service, not karma. During our life together this time, Michael was the stimulus behind the person I became. Through his death, Michael helped me with the service I now provide. In my counseling practice when I have a client raw with the gut-wrenching pain of losing a child, I could say, "I understand, you are not alone and you can get through this." It really depends on how willing we are to look at the experience from a different perspective. My friend Mary's daughter died when she was six months old. Mary shared with me that as she searched for answers to the unexplainable, the pain and the sorrow, she was led to a new way of life, a new way of thinking. She has been on the path of spiritual growth and service for decades and this began because of her daughter's death.

We are in the dying process as is all life from the moment of our birth. All one needs to do is look at the human body right now—wherever you are in the cycle of this incarnation. Chronologically are you closer to your birth or your death? Then go back and look at pictures of when you were a child, an adolescent, a young adult to the age you are now. Focus on how the body has changed. Nothing is stagnant—energy is motion.

With awareness and consciousness, there is no denying that the only thing constant is change. Unfortunately, many people, rather than embracing change, resist it and in resisting change create suffering. Understanding that death is the portal to the next experience of life allows us to accept and even embrace change.

Everything has a shelf life on this organic planet. In accepting this reality, we then can treasure the present moment and enjoy the ride until it is time for us to return Home, to Source, to God.

FEAR OF DEATH

∞

Why are people frightened by death? The unknown is the obvious answer—the other, it is my contention, is what we have been told, conditioned to believe what happens after death which is taught in multiple forms and ways by our religions. A prevalent emotion in Western religion is fear. The opposite of love is fear—the opposite end of the continuum from love. If death was understood for what it is—a portal to the next level of life—there would be no fear. Many Indian tribes knew and honored this. When an elder knew (or perhaps decided) to pass on—they walked away from the tribe and did pass. The physical form ends as the Spirit energy leaves. God is Love and our Spirit returns to this Love where there is no room for judgment.

Is it the dying, the manner in which we die, or the unknown, that causes the most fear? We know that life on this planet is fragile and most of us have experienced the sudden death and/or painful death of someone we love. It is overwhelming and yet many of us have seen a peace and surrender come over the person in that state. In fact, if we look back at the unexpected death of someone we love, we may realize that the inner Spirit had a knowing, though not necessarily the physical person, the mind and intellect. Many people have had the experience of seeing peace in the eyes of loved ones prior to their passage. I had the privilege of being with my husband Gary as he sat on the beach looking out over the ocean at the clear, blue sky with his eyes brilliant, sparkling in awe, and his smile radiant before he passed.

So, what to do—don't resist, be flexible and imagine the death of the physical body that you fear. How often have you come across people whose greatest fear is cancer, ending up in a nursing home or dying from an accident, and then it happens? Do we create the future by focusing on it and in this case fear? Or does the inner Spirit already know how we have chosen to go back to Source? Ask yourself that question in the context of understanding our personal responsibility and choices we made prior to incarnating. Then, trust and let it go because it is what it is.

My friend Wendy shared a very personal experience with me about the power of surrender. I asked and she agreed to share with you this experience.

> *"Our daughter was a 16 year old foreign exchange student in New Zealand when she died in an*

automobile accident along with three other members of her host family. I remember staying in the house during most of the Christmas holidays, not venturing out at all. Finally the well- meaning, but draining condolences of visitors, friends and family; the grief and depression; the feeling that I must be strong for my husband and son; and the overcast weather were too much for me. I sat down and said to God, "I can't take anymore. Help me!" Then quickly a peace and calmness filled my being. I knew as difficult as our loss was we would move on in our lives without her, but with one another and God as our strength and support."

If we can accept and learn to die while we are living, if we can go through the stages of loss, of mourning the death of the physical body while we are alive, would that not free us to live more fully in the present moment?

RELATIONSHIPS CHANGE

∞

I t is interesting as we ponder and observe, how do people relate? The faces of relationship vary in such diversity and change throughout our lives. From birth to death we connect, disconnect, magnify, and diminish our connections to the initial core group that we are born into. In some cases, the connection to parents remains somewhat consistent throughout our life; in other cases that relationship shatters quickly; in other situations, parents die, divorce, change partners as our relationship to our parents continues to flux, change and modify.

Now look at this same concept with siblings, cousins, aunts, uncles—whatever the structure is called, family, tribe, community—whatever model it takes. Now look at it as it expands in our lives to community, church, school, associations, etc. These relationships vibrate at different levels of energy. The energy is sometimes high, sometimes low, sometimes positive and sometimes negative. What do all of these have in common? They exist for a while and then end on this plane. Where did they come from? Why did they last for a while or not?

Prior to our birth in form we choose the experience to live, to learn, to balance karma, to teach and to serve. There is no way of knowing from the onset the purpose of any particular relationship we experience and encounter; however, as we become conscious, as our awareness increases, we can see the value of these relationships, especially the most significant and primary. We can look back at the tapestry that formed in awe, inspiration and gratitude. This then leads to peace and acceptance when the relationship is over this time, in this form, on planet earth. **Death is the End of an Incarnation, not a Relationship.**

RELATIONSHIPS ASSIST

∞

Many enlightened, conscious Spirits will attest and have attested to the ongoing awareness and connection to loved ones who have passed into transition, have left the physical plane. It is these individuals that allowed themselves to become free of the fear of dying, free to explore the tenets they have been taught or acculturated with, to go in peace to continued experiences in life.

Karen is my very close cousin—our fathers were brothers. Karen is willing to share her experience of assistance and on-going communication with her Dad.

> *"I believe death is the beginning of something else. And I believe that our friends and relatives who have died still watch over us. For example, I was very close to my father and I often felt his presence after he died. I worked at a hospital that was located high on a hill. My house was two miles*

away in the valley below. One day, while I was at work, it began to snow. I had meetings well into the evening and by the time I started home, it was cold, wet, snowy and slippery. As I started driving down the hill, my biggest concern was the sharp right turn and then the sharp left turn at the bottom of the hill before the road flattened out in the valley. I was very nervous as I inched my way down the slippery slope. As I got closer to the bottom, I looked to my right and saw my Dad sitting there— eyes straight ahead—looking like he always did when HE was driving. He told me to down shift to first gear, keep my foot OFF the brake, and slowly make the right turn. I did so but I slid slightly as we approached the left turn. He told me not to panic—that I had control of the car and we were almost home. I felt his comforting presence, made it through both turns, and got home safely. My Dad was with me that night as he always is—especially in times of trouble."

RELATIONSHIPS CONTINUE

∞

I f you take the time to examine past relationships in your life, without judgment, you will see the ebb and flow, the value of all of them as balance, a learning experience, a teacher, a service you provided, etc. Then, look at how they ended, how you drifted apart once the purpose was served. This becomes more understandable later in life for individuals reaching fifty years old or more in this life than for younger vibrating spirits. It is interesting and worth examining how these relationships end. If you can think of that experience this time in this life with no negative emotions but rather gratitude, you'll have a sense of peace about the experience with this Spirit in form this time.

In a lifetime, in every life there is work to be done, service to be given, love to give and to experience. We are born into flesh to have the vehicle we need to experience this adventure, this life. As the body develops and experiences the stages of growth, each phase offers opportunity, challenges and experiences.

It is our job to embrace these experiences with Love and Gratitude for what they bring us. Ponder on this—it is not what happens, but how we Respond to what happens. We are co-creators of our Life and choose from a higher awareness these experiences. **Embrace Them, Live Them.**

It is okay if these concepts don't resonate with you, if you think it is just a nice comforting story. If you aren't ready to consider these universal truths, that is okay. The collective consciousness of this planet fights against these truths. The ideas that we are responsible for our lives and that we are co-creators in designing the experiences, the balance of karma, the learning prior to coming to human form is scary for many humans. It pulls the rug out from under them because in resonating with these truths, they can no longer be victims; they can no longer engage in the blame game; they can no longer justify their participation in resonating with the lower frequencies of fear, envy, jealousy, hate, guilt, holding grudges and all the lower frequencies that while vibrating with them justifies their perception of personal worth, class and control over others. It is pretty scary, if that's all you know, to consider reframing everything you've been taught and believe and focus on the purpose in life to be only **Love** and **Service**.

Great masters, spiritual teachers and healers are bringing to the consciousness of humans the importance of dying while you are alive this time on this plane. This concept is not only difficult, but almost impossible for the masses to accept—yet— but how they can is by communication with the Spirit world of God. The avatars of past cultures communicated between planes. The respect for life, for the dying process was paramount in their knowing that goes beyond belief. As a race, we lost this and to advance in awareness and consciousness we need to become one with this universal truth.

The life energy that always was and always will be that comes from Source or call it Universal Intelligence, Atman, God—know that it dwells in you and you have chosen an opportunity to express life in your current physical form—this beautiful vehicle we call our body.

Many us have had and will continue to have communication with and assistance from our loved ones who have gone home before us. I will end this section by sharing experiences, just two of the many I have had, after my son died in 1988 and my husband in 2006.

> *"Michael was sixteen when he died suddenly in an automobile accident twenty four years ago. That first year was a complete blur and I felt nothing. In fact, I never thought I would be able to feel again. I stayed in the same townhouse and went through the motions of life for a couple of years. Then unexpectedly I had an overwhelming desire*

to move. I was able to find another townhouse in a weekend in the northwest suburbs of Philadelphia. Though it was less than an hour away, it was a very different area from where Michael and I lived.

One night shortly after I settled in, I woke up suddenly and knew I needed to go downstairs. I went into my office which was slightly lit from the outside street lamp. I felt a presence behind me, it was Michael. He was the same size and build as he was when he died. His body was not solid but ethereal, a brilliant white light that filled the room. He reached out his hands and took my hands then turned and walked into the living room. I followed him and we sat on the sofa and talked, not with words—it is very hard to explain—but with thoughts, with a knowing. He shared a lot, but the most important was that he finally got me to move and now I needed to move on with my life because I had a lot to do. Then just like he appeared, he faded away.

Gary and I loved Mexico and vacationed there often. We loved Cancun and the Rivera Maya so much that we purchased beautiful beach front timeshare villas that would allow us to vacation in Mexico for at least six weeks annually once we retired. In the meantime, we would spend two weeks in Mexico every October. In October 2006, the day we were celebrating our wedding anniversary, Gary died on the beach in front of our villa and a few feet away from where we were married. After a gut wrenching year of experiencing the stages of loss and healing, I returned alone to Mexico. I had to make a decision about whether Mexico would continue to be part of my life or if I should sell the villas. When I arrived at our villa, I was greeted by this beautiful Monarch butterfly flying around. I sat down and cried because of Gary's connection to butterflies. Gary had a love for butterflies and they had a love for him. They were always around him. I loved when a butterfly would rest on Gary's hand, book or shoulder when we'd be reading outside on summer evenings. For the next three days as I experienced a range of emotions trying to decide what to do, the butterfly stayed. I would leave the sliding glass door open, but it didn't matter, the butterfly stayed. Towards the evening of the third day when I returned to the villa, the butterfly had stopped flying and lay on the marble shower floor. I wasn't sure if it was still alive, but decided to pick it up with a washcloth and put it on the balcony. I sat on the balcony with the butterfly on the floor not moving, thinking about the decision I had to make. After about a half hour, I walked to the railing and looked at the magnificent blue water and said to myself, "I love it here, I have wonderful memories, and I am going to continue coming here." As I went to sit down, the butterfly gingerly flapped a wing and then slowly flew away. There is no doubt in my mind, not only about what happened, but how I felt about what happened, that through that butterfly my husband helped me make the decision. The decision was to keep the timeshare villas. Since Gary died, every October I go back to Mexico to relax, enjoy and remember how blessed I am.

When I came home, I needed to have a bracelet repaired that I didn't get to before I went to Mexico. Gary loved to buy me jewelry and I especially loved jewelry with gemstones. The last piece he had bought me was a blue topaz ring framed with peridots. I hadn't bought any jewelry since. We had a special jeweler who loved his work especially in re-designing jewelry from old estate pieces. When I stopped by the store to drop off my bracelet, I glanced down at the display. There was a butterfly necklace (one of a kind) with wings of blue topaz and peridot gemstones. It was a perfect match for *my ring and before I did anything, the thought came (from Gary), "Buy it it's yours" and I did."*

We can communicate with those we love that have passed and sometimes even better, without human emotions and issues interfering with our communication. To accept anything, understanding is the first step. In essence, our consciousness needs to understand that it is Spirit and the form that Spirit takes changes from lifetime to lifetime. Spirit chooses to explore, learn and experience through form. That is how it works.

PART THREE

∞

WHAT DO WE NEED TO UNDERSTAND?

REINCARNATION
RELIGION & CULTURE
FAMILY & RELATIONSHIPS
IMPERMANENCE
LOVE & PEACE

REINCARNATION

To be aware of the universal truth of reincarnation is essential. This concept cannot be fully realized intellectually. It must be felt. Consider—why do humans become attracted or repelled to each other? Unless someone is living totally unconsciously, the experience of attraction, repulsion or indifference when we encounter each other happens. Consider why and the thought comes as reincarnation. My Spirit was incarnate (physical body) at another time and perhaps another dimension when it had encountered and been connected or not with this other Spirit.

For most religions, reincarnation is a cornerstone of the belief system. This manuscript is not about trying to convince anyone about reincarnation. Many books have been written on this subject; in fact, if you Google reincarnation there are over eighteen million references. You will resonate with this truth or not.

Karma is neither good nor bad: it is cause and effect, choice and consequence, action and reaction. Based on the intention and motivation of our choices, karma is positive or negative—very different than good or bad.

The positive and the negative are at opposite ends of the continuum. The balance is at center, the core. Our job as human beings is to balance the negative and positive within us. In entering this incarnation, the positive and negative are present in Spirit. Our manifestation in form is the awakening of consciousness, the realization that life as we know it is a choice made in Spirit so that the consciousness that we are can experience all that form allows. It cannot be otherwise. The Spirit is experiencing, learning, balancing all previous incarnations each time it comes into form. On the Spirit plane our life is designed for the human experience that we co-create.

RELIGION & CULTURE

∞

There is confusion on earth because humans have been given such conflicting information from various forms of ideology and belief systems. If we look at all religions, dogma, political systems, cultural mores, we can connect the dots to understand universal truth. What is it? We come from Spirit—the formless—into form to experience life on planet earth. When the experience is complete we return to formless, to God, to Source, to Universal Intelligence. Call it whatever you want to call it.

Why don't we resonate with this universal truth? Because we have been taught differently. No religion, ideology or law has the power to reduce universal laws to fit into a construct that says, "This is the only way. We are right." The reality is that as you become awake, aware and conscious, you can choose to vibrate with the higher frequencies or the lower frequencies. It is your choice. Feel what it feels like when you choose the higher or lower frequencies. Then you will know.

This is not a belief. It is a knowing and when you know you cannot not know.

The question is: "Where did I come from and where am I going?" The Spirit comes from Source, God, and returns to Source, God. Religion can serve as a foundation, not of rules, but a design, a pattern of human conduct towards humans and all living things.....Love of God, of Oneself, of thy Neighbor. Is that not the essence, the beginning of understanding the essence of Love, of God, of Source in everything? Knowing this truth, we cannot participate in lying, cheating, killing, blaming—any of the lower frequencies. Once we understand this, we begin to move away from the human drama and the ego. We cease to judge anything including suffering because we have no way of knowing if it is karmic balance, karmic creation or service.

It is a violation in human interaction to judge anyone's life experience. We simply have absolutely no way of knowing another person's purpose. As we are co-creators in the blueprint of the life we are coming to earth to experience, there could be one or many purposes and reasons. Some include learning, service, balancing karma and others that we don't know about.

FAMILY & RELATIONSHIPS

amily—what is that and why? The family we are born into is the family of karma and service. Sometimes we reincarnate into a family where the purpose is service to each other; however, more often than not, the family we choose to be born into gives us an opportunity to balance karma from previous lives together. Spirits choose to experience and explore on many levels, but the exploring is rarely with the biological family. And why is that? It is because of the law of karma—cause and effect, choice and consequences. Generally speaking, we choose to reincarnate with the energy of those we have had experiences with in past lives. The multitudes of incarnations are a balancing of the growth, expansion and awareness of our Spirit consciousness. It may sound like a very complicated process, but it really isn't.

To make the concept of karmic balance from lifetime to lifetime simple, let's look at an example of this process of balancing and creating karma. A woman (let's call her Mary) and a man (let's call him John) experienced lifetimes together. In a past life, John was Mary's husband who loved, took care of her, and honored her. They had a joyous incarnation. After that incarnation John reincarnates a number of times without Mary, but in those incarnations, he was not the loving, kind vibration that Mary knew. In those incarnations he resonated with negative frequencies and discarded the positive. In Spirit form prior to reincarnating again to earth, John with the assistance of his guides decides to combine a number of incarnations to balance his previous negative incarnations. In his choice from Spirit awareness, he decides to incarnate as a disabled, mentally challenged child. For him to do that, he needs a mother who would understand, accept this role and help him with basic survival needs. He chooses Mary, his previous wife, to assist him in balancing his karma. Now here's the catch, John chooses Mary and she has the opportunity to balance karma, the positiveness and love she experienced with John in their last life on earth. Karma is neither good nor bad, it just is—it is universal law—As Above So Below.

Mary, in Spirit form prior to reincarnating, designed the blueprint for the life she would experience and part of it was to assist him and balance karma. Mary chose to do this, and then volition sets in, free will, because memory of choice in Spirit form negates karmic balance. Now, the child is born through her. If Mary accepts, loves, nurtures this disabled child, she is balancing karma. If she doesn't, when this child is born through her, Mary not only loses the opportunity to balance her karma with John, but she potentially can create more karma. He may even balance additional karma by her rejection.

In physical form all relationships end. This is the reality for humans as well as all life forms. Knowing this, does it not make sense and encourage us to look at that reality rather than avoid it, hoping it won't happen. So, let's look at it and we begin with why relationships are formed. Ask yourself that question. Why am I attracted to someone and not someone else? What is it that draws me?

Romantic love is the most elementary form of love, but it is a beginning, enjoyable and fun because of the aliveness we experience and the potential it offers. See it for what it is and realize that our form is the vehicle that gives us the opportunity to have this experience. Then see what happens. As every great love knows, this initial physical love will either mature to an advanced love with contentment and peace or it will end.

Love manifests in many different forms and these are experienced by us at different times during this earthly incarnation. In the end we know that Love is vibrating with the higher vibrations, the higher energies of service, generosity, non-judgment, caring, compassion, kindness and being available to each other, to support each other on this trip of earthly experiences.

IMPERMANENCE

To realize the impermanence of everything is freeing. There is no more correlation between what I have and what I want. Now it is all about Spirit. The value of material wealth has only one purpose and that is to free the Spirit from the mundane needs for survival so that your focus can be serving—serving yourself in awareness and consciousness and serving each other and all living things.

The Spirit knows the truth—Source—where it came from and where it is going in this space we call time that doesn't exist. As the Spirit enters the earth plane, it has designed the opportunities it wants to experience and learn and the opportunities to balance karma from previous incarnations. This is the truth and in hearing this, the Spirit will resonate. Is it resonating, making sense? It will not resonate with this truth if ego gets involved. If it doesn't resonate, it is because ego got in the way. Ego demands attention, praise and fights the truth. The truth is that everything that happens has Purpose, Design and Love.

Detachment is so important. Let's look at an example, a person who is worried about her things, "What will happen to my material possessions when I die?" The thought of her accumulations not being valued or taken care of is distressing. Why would anyone be concerned about "things" when their Spirit leaves this plane of existence? **It is identification with form that causes pain**. The truth is we come to earth with nothing and we leave with nothing. Everything is recycled. The purpose of material possessions is to assist us in experiencing and enjoying the Earth plane during our time here in form. **Material possessions serve us, not the other way around.**

LOVE & PEACE

L ove is the essence of Life and where there is Love there is Peace. When Love is not present conflict arises and in conflict there is duality, suffering and fear. When are we at Peace? We are at Peace when we are vibrating in Love, Truth and Service.

Where is Peace? How can anyone be at Peace in the insane conditions and mind of the human race? Go back, even in thought and try to remember when you felt at peace—remember the details—remember the moment. I am not talking about happiness, I am talking about Peace. You will know what I mean by going back and looking at and feeling the experience, however brief, that made you feel peace, joy—the higher frequencies. Was it in seeing your child for the first time or watching that child sleep? Was it looking in the eyes of someone you loved? Was it the first time you saw the ocean or realized the majesty of a sunrise or sunset?

Go deep and remember...when you do, you realize that it was **Love**. It was realizing something greater than yourself that gave you that feeling of **Peace Profound**. Then ask yourself, can I experience this peace continuously? The answer is "**Yes**" if you live in a continuous state of **Gratitude** and if you choose to vibrate with the higher frequencies of love, generosity, forgiveness, service. The feeling of Peace departs when we vibrate with the lower frequencies of jealousy, fear, hate, control and competition.

PART FOUR

∞

WHAT CAN WE DO?

FOCUS ON THE PRESENT MOMENT
STAGES OF LOSS—
THE MOURNING PROCESS
HEALING
CELEBRATING LIFE & RITUALS
HOW TO AVOID CREATING
NEGATIVE KARMA

FOCUS ON THE PRESENT MOMENT

∞

Life as we know it is not Life. It is an illusion. The core of Life is essence. Order in life reflects the order in the universe. As we try to figure out the whys, we only get more whys because our vision and ability to understand on planet earth is limited, and needs to be. If there is no Life as we know it, then there is no Death. One cannot exist without the other. Once that concept penetrates your whole being, Fear is gone.

So what is Real? The Present Moment is our only reality. It is the portal through which we can find Peace, Joy, and Awareness that leads to the expansion of our Consciousness. Yesterday is gone, tomorrow hasn't happened and focusing on either can cause pain, suffering and disappointment. Having something to look forward to, like a vacation, is a pleasant part of being a human. The important thing to remember is **"Stay Detached"** because then if the vacation gets cancelled, you'll avoid reacting negatively and feeling negative emotions. Plan like you will Live forever. Live like you will Die immediately. **There is only the Present Moment, the Now.**

Consider this for a moment. Each night when we go to sleep we face the unknown. Where is our consciousness, our life force, our awareness as we sleep? Then we leave the state of sleep to begin again a new day. Why in the consciousness of being awake, moving through our day are we okay and not fearful of death? Is it because we are so focused on doing that we distract ourselves enough to lower our awareness that at any moment we could die? And then, if we get that call that someone we know has died or a massive tragedy like 9/11 has happened, we become paralyzed by the realization that the human life form is fragile and only exists in the present moment. Sometimes someone we love takes their time dying to give us time to adjust. Usually this is a service to us. Is it not true that we can physically die at any moment? Have we not seen the fragility of life in the physical body? So, what to do?

Go deep and begin to explore the meaning of death. The opposite of death is not life because in physical death our life energy, our life force, our Spirit, continues though in another dimension unknown to us. **The opposite of Death is Birth**. The flow of energy—synchronicity—all comes together when Awareness and Consciousness remain present. When you are drawn into drama, into conflict, know that it is a distraction created by human ego. It is our ego that makes us think that life is about possessions, attachments, competition and control.

STAGES OF LOSS—THE
MOURNING PROCESS

∞

Much has been written about the stages of loss. Elisabeth Kubler-Ross, a pioneer in the field of Death & Dying, provides a model to assist us in understanding the emotions, the feelings, that arise when relationships end through physical death on the Earth Plane. The stages of loss in the mourning process applies to any loss we sustain. Our focus here is on loss through death, but the same human emotional responses apply to whatever we perceive as a loss such as health, home, job, reputation, aging process, etc. What determines the intensity of the emotions we experience through a loss is determined by our perception of the significance of the loss. For example, let's say we have an accident that requires a hospital stay, surgery and rehabilitation. We will have emotional responses to the accident, but because we survived and healed, the Reactions aren't as intense as they would have been had the accident resulted in a loss of limb or ongoing disability.

Knowing the stages of loss, of what to expect, helps us understand what we will go through and need to go through to heal. The process begins with Shock and Denial. Healing is complete when we are able to Accept the loss.

When we get a phone call that someone we know has died, our first Reaction is Shock and Denial. The same would be true if our physician diagnosed us with cancer. If the call about the person that died is a relative whom we met once and lived on the other side of the country, the intensity of our shock and denial would be minimum compared to our Reaction if the call was about our child in an accident. The comparison is the same with the diagnosis of cancer—very early stages, treatable and curable, versus the final stage of pancreatic cancer.

After Shock and Denial, we start Bargaining: "If I do this, then maybe this nightmare will go away." An example of the Bargaining stage is a wife telling her husband, "The children are raised so now the marriage is over and I am leaving you." After the Shock and Denial, his bargaining could involve asking her to give him another chance. How can I change so you won't leave me? What do I need to do? These are all Bargaining attempts to avoid dealing with the loss.

The next stages are not in any order. They are Depression, Withdrawal, Anger and Guilt. On any given day through the process of mourning, these emotions will come and go, day by day and week by week. Sometimes you will spend days crying. Other times you might be so angry that you'll give up on God. These emotions will surface when you least expect them like being in the grocery store after your husband died and reaching for his favorite snack. Then you have to do everything to contain yourself from losing it and breaking down in tears right there in the aisle.

Finally, the last stage of mourning is Acceptance. This is the final stage in mourning all losses. The way you know that you have accepted the loss is by your emotional response when you think about the person who died. This does not mean that you will not cry when you hear that particular song that reminds you of your loss. What it means is the gut-wrenching pain is gone. In fact, the tears become tears of gratitude for what you had experienced with your loved one. You take that moment and remember, and then go on with your life. We honor our loved ones who have passed by not taking their death personally. Our loved ones want us to continue to enjoy the joys and pleasures that planet earth offers us.

If we are willing to think about loss and accept it as part of life, everything changes because our relationships change. It's called Unconditional Love. In the present moment we appreciate and honor the people with whom we are sharing this Earthly experience. As we age, and deal with deaths of close relatives and friends, we are given more opportunities to emotionally deal with our own mortality. As difficult as it is, we need to experience the stages of loss and not get stuck in the process. If we resist the process of healing, if we become a victim and take the loss personally, it will affect everything we do going forward in our life. As painful as it is, we need to feel the emotions to Heal.

Our culture has a difficult time dealing with Mourning, with Grieving and that is unfortunate. In understanding the stages of loss, it is very important to know that what you are feeling is okay—feelings are not right or wrong, they just are. The mourning process is very personal and no one should ever judge the way another person is grieving. Sometimes the process has to be delayed as it was for me when my husband died. Gary was a Chiropractor. His patients were deeply affected by his sudden death. The very least I could do for them was transition their care to another Chiropractor and manage his practice until I could sell it to the right owner. It took six months and then I was able to begin my mourning process.

If you have the courage to live through the gut-wrenching mourning, the feelings of loss, you are now ready to Heal. If you don't heal a loss, the next loss that you experience brings back the previous loss even stronger. It opens up the wound that hasn't healed making the new loss even more painful.

Unconditional Love is required to accept Death. Understand that every physical relationship on this planet ends. Understanding leads to the Awareness that when you Love Unconditionally, **LOVE NEVER DIES.**

HEALING

∞

There are many ways that we can heal from any loss, but we can't even start the process unless we have the courage to go through the stages of loss. One of the fears we have in healing is that in time we will forget the smile, the touch, the laugh of our loved one. And actually that is partly true. As our loved one goes on to the next level of life and experience, we start forgetting things about them and we can get upset and feel we are dishonoring our beloved. It is time to get past that again with awareness and by resonating with truth. Our loved ones (with the awareness they now have) love us unconditionally; staying stuck rather than enjoying the rest of our experience on planet earth is simply not an option and does not honor our loved ones.

How do we go on with our life and still honor our loved ones? By _Responding_ to what has happened, not _Reacting_. The difference is: a Response is taking Action, a Reaction is Acting Out. Responding appropriately can only happen after the mourning process is complete. A person's Reactions could manifest as being the victim or using the death as an excuse to abdicate one's personal responsibility to continue pursuing one's purpose in life. You will know if you are Responding or Reacting by how you feel. If you are feeling at Peace, you are Responding; if you are feeling stuck, you are Reacting.

Responding requires Action and the Action leads to Healing. There are many positive ways of Responding. For some it might be joining a support group like Compassionate Friends that focuses on helping parents heal after the death of a child. For others it might be seeing a counselor, accessing the services of Hospice or reassessing the priorities of life.

Some of our Responses are life changing and sometimes they are small, but significant. For example, as I was healing from Michael's death, one of the things that really bothered me was, when I'd meet someone new, soon the person would ask, "Do you have any children?" I wanted to say yes, but almost always that response resulted in the person getting upset or making an inappropriate comment like "You are young enough to have more children." The action I took to deal with this was to go away to an island by myself where I could meet people I probably would never see again. When the question came up, my response was "Yes, I had a son, but he died." Since I didn't know the person, I had no problem Responding to any inappropriate remarks. By practicing on a lot of people that week, I learned that I could and would always acknowledge Michael when that question is asked. And if the person got upset—well, they asked the question. By taking this action in my healing process, I was able to and continue to Respond to inappropriate (though probably well-meaning) remarks without an emotional Reaction.

Sometimes the Response to death is huge and ongoing for healing to occur. Such was the case of my dear friend Lynn. She offered to share her story about what she did to help heal from the loss of her only nephew, Ryan.

> "We were very excited when my sister told the family that she was pregnant. This would be the first grandchild for my mom, as I don't have any children. On October 6, 2000, Ryan Michael Chute was born.
>
> Everything seemed fine but then around Christmas, my sister noticed some bruising on Ryan and he wasn't eating. She took him to the doctors and tests were ordered. In January 2001, Ryan was diagnosed with AML, Acute Myelogenous Leukemia. He unfortunately had the rare type, which has a very low survival rate.

All the questions that everyone asks themselves, we were asking. When there are no answers, you turn to your belief systems along with the angels and praying. Long-distance prayer and talking on the phone was a daily occurrence. Continuing to ask the questions of "why?" and "what does this mean?" weighed heavily on my mind.

As the days went on Ryan was in and out of the hospital and shortly after Ryan's diagnosis, probably in the spring, I received a flyer in the mail. I usually throw them away, but this one attracted my attention. It was from the Leukemia and Lymphoma Society. They have a program called Team in Training and by running or walking a marathon you could raise money to help patients with leukemia. Curious and now personally connected, I went to the informational meeting. In November 2001, I completed my first marathon in Bermuda and with the help of family and friends was able to raise over $7,000 for The Leukemia and Lymphoma Society. At the same time Ryan was being treating at MD Anderson Cancer Center in Houston, Texas, participating in a clinical trial.

In January 2002, at 15 months of age, Ryan died. At that time I knew where my path would lead. I became personally involved with the local Chapter of LLS and committed to raise funds and do one marathon for every month of his life.

On January 7, 2012 I completed my 15th marathon. Up to then I had raised over $80,000 for the Leukemia and Lymphoma Society. I have been actively involved and remain on the Board of Trustees for the Chapter, have helped in the patient services program and been a member of the advocacy committee. I have also been a coach / mentor for the Team in Training program.

On a bright note, during the 15 events, I could ALWAYS count on my "angel" to watch over me, as it NEVER rained, nor did I encounter bad weather. The team has a saying, "If Lynn is doing an event, don't worry about the weather, it will be fine. Ryan, our weather angel, is watching over us." We love and miss you!!!"

Realize that as you are healing so are those you love and anyone affected by the loss of your loved one. One of the first questions I ask a client who comes to me for grief counseling is, "Who abandoned you?" Then with wide and teary eyes, he or she says how did you know? I do the best I can to help them understand that they are abandoned because of the fear, conflicts, issues and grief, the person (s) who have abandoned them are going through and that has nothing to do with them. Is it fair, **No**—should the person experiencing the greatest loss have the support of those they thought loved them and would be there for them—**YES, of course**—but everyone's ability of love, be there for you and support you during your loss depends on their awareness and consciousness. I've worked through this process myself and help my clients work through it so they do not get stuck in the stages of loss that delay their healing process.

Children and adolescents are especially vulnerable when someone they love dies, because of their lack of life experience. Fortunately there are many books available today to help parents assist their children in dealing with the fear of death and the aftermath of the death of those they love. Michael's peers were devastated when he died and what helped them was knowing they could come to my home anytime and talk. Teachers were wonderful by having Michael's friends write me letters telling me what Michael meant to them. I still cherish those letters. For Danine, Michael's girlfriend, part of her healing process was dedicating the song she sang at the high school's spring recital (The Rose) to Michael.

For each of us, the process of Healing is different and yet similar. It may take months, it may take years, it may take a decade, but it will occur if we want to Heal and if we honor the process.

CELEBRATING LIFE & RITUALS

∞

C elebrating Life is honoring Oneself, God and those We Love. Many things in life are difficult and the way to balance the difficult times and events of our lives is to Celebrate Life and the Joy it brings anytime we can. Striving for Balance is essential to having a wonderful life. Balance in every area and aspect of our lives—Physically, Spiritually, Mentally, Emotionally, Psychologically, Socially etc.

Laughter, fun, enjoyment should be part of each day. Anyone who knows me, knows I play hard, very hard, and I love it. I dance—I'm a dancer—one of the many things I do for fun. I need to really play (as do you) to balance the intensity of the work I do, the service I provide. Everyone needs to play, to balance, because there is no such thing as a life without suffering, disappointment, betrayal, pain,—and playing is the balance.

To fully enjoy life, we need to choose lifestyle activities that honor our Body, Mind and Spirit. Our energy, our life force needs to flow for us to reach our maximum potential. Each person has to decide what works for them. For me my lifestyle choices include being subluxation free through Chiropractic adjustments, Meditation, Massage, Yoga and Tai Chi. Whatever works for you is what matters. Make the choices that contribute to the celebration of Your Life.

Rituals are a form of celebration that exist in all cultures and religions. There are rituals for everything and anything that is part of existence on this planet. Rituals serve as the string that connects and unites individuals, families, communities and nations. They have purpose and span the continuum from joy to sorrow.

Rituals surrounding death are important for those who remain and sometimes for the dying, as was the situation with my friend Phyllis' Dad. He was very clear that he didn't want any type of service, funeral, when he died. His position was that people could visit him, and enjoy his company while he was alive, not dead. His family honored this and the day before he was to be transported to hospice, his family had the ritual celebration of his life. Phyllis' Dad was Italian and the food and wine flowed—every kind imaginable. There was dancing, laughter and singing. This ritual celebrated for one last time a life lived in love and with family. How wonderful for the children and the grandchildren to participate in the celebration of life with no fear of death.

Most rituals surrounding death occur after the person dies. These rituals (funerals, memorials, whatever form they take) are for the living. They bring comfort, closure and support. One needs to experience the death of someone very close to realize the significance of the death ritual. Though there is sadness because of the loss of the physical person, the ritual can be comforting and peaceful if fear is not part of the process.

All cultures have their death rituals that bring comfort to those left behind. When my husband died suddenly in Mexico (at our home away from home), our Mexican friends were deeply affected. Nathan, our dearest friend, asked me for the honor of dressing Gary before his body went back to the states. I had never heard of this ritual and Nathan explained to me that his family and the Mexican people always want to look their best. The honor of dressing the body of a loved one after they died was given to the eldest member of the family—male or female, it didn't matter. Nathan knew how much Gary loved Mexico, the people, the culture and felt Gary should be dressed according to their ritual. I was honored, as I knew Gary would be, that Nathan asked to do this and did—a memory I will always treasure.

My Dad's death is an example of how we can teach our children not to fear death. My son Michael was my Dad's only grandchild. They were very close. The night before Dad died they were up late playing. My Dad died in his sleep. Michael was raised with the universal truths that are presented in this manuscript. Prior to the funeral director transporting my Dad's body, I brought Michael (who was eight years old at the time) into the bedroom to see Dziadek (that is Polish for Grandfather), to see how peaceful death is, to touch him and to say good bye. Michael had no fear of death because he was raised knowing that death is a natural part of life.

We can create whatever rituals we want to give us comfort and help us stay connected to those we love. I was born and raised as Catholic, a Polish Catholic, with a ritual that does exactly that on Christmas Eve called Wigilia. The family comes together to share a traditional Polish meal. At the table there is an empty plate to remind us of those who have died. Prior to our meal we pray and remember those who are no longer with us— and sometimes we cry, especially if a loved one passed in the preceding year. Then we break the wafer wishing each other health and happiness in the upcoming year. The memory of these Wigilias stay in my heart as I continue to celebrate Wigilia every Christmas Eve. I especially remember one Wigilia when four generations of my family were present—Cioci Rosie, her son Bobby, his son Robbie, and his daughter Amanda— Mother to

Son to Grandson to Great Granddaughter—that is the flow of life, the ongoing evolution of family, that is how we are all connected in Love.

Though Cioci Rosie is not physically with us, when my dear cousins Bobby and his wife, Elaine celebrate Wigilia their three children and spouses, and ten grandchildren are present to celebrate their lives and the lives of those who have passed and who they know will be with them again.

HOW TO AVOID CREATING
NEGATIVE KARMA

∞

On the earth plane as on the cosmic plane, we live by laws, "As Above So Below."

For every Choice there is a Consequence, for every Action there is a Reaction, for every Cause there is an Effect. The laws simply provide a blueprint to assist us in the decisions we make. There is and always has to be congruence with universal law and mundane law.

When we incarnate to the earth plane in a state of amnesia, we begin a human experience with the great gift of choice. Through our choices the goal is to Love and Serve and in that process learn, experience and balance karma. We could waste an entire incarnation by making wrong choices and creating negative karma.

To Avoid Creating Negative Karma:

- ✓ Be impeccable with your word, honesty—never lie
- ✓ No violence or abuse ever
- ✓ Never take advantage of someone lesser than you
- ✓ Follow the rules of your society and culture as you understand and accept them

This foundation of FOUR are the guidelines for congruent human choice and behavior. Our relationship to Ourselves, God and Each Other should help us to follow these guidelines. Unfortunately this is not always the case.

The most important relationship we have is the one we have with our self. We cannot give what we do not have. We need to love ourselves, be kind, gentle, compassionate and forgiving to ourselves at all times. When we fail, we learn, then move on without judgment or criticism. These are the characteristics of God, of Universal Intelligence and of Innate Intelligence—The God within us. This is the way we should interact with our fellow human beings. Even when it isn't achievable in some of our relationships, it is the goal worth striving for.

During our human experience there are times when we need to end a relationship. As we interact with each other in relationships, we are either adding to or taking away from the other person. If the relationship vibrates with the frequencies of love, generosity, compassion, understanding, all of the positive emotions, the relationship is healthy and supports us with our life purpose. If the relationship vibrates with the frequencies of fear, hate, jealousy, greed and all of the negative emotions, the relationship is toxic. We cannot be in a growth-producing relationship and a toxic one at the same time. Change is part of relationships and any relationship can change from loving and supportive to toxic.

When someone who has low energy and vibration is in your presence, he or she can sap your energy. It doesn't mean that they are negative, it just means the relationship is not working for you at this time. When you realize that someone is draining you, be still and surround yourself with light and petition to your higher Source to be surrounded by the positive energy being projected to you from Universal Intelligence. You will feel peaceful, lighter, or not. If not, consider minimizing your time with that person, even to the point of having to end the physical, mundane relationship and then send that person Love and Peace.

Anger, deception, manipulation and control are indicators of a toxic relationship. These relationships do not honor your Spirit or your Life. If the relationship was once positive, loving and caring, ending it is very painful and the mourning process needs to happen. It is helpful to give thanks for what you once had and then let it go, knowing that every relationship on the earth plane ends.

On this planet humans hurt humans and can cause each other pain. Sometimes this is deliberate, at other times it is a reaction to insecurity, lack of self-confidence and self-esteem. One can never balance negativity by attack, confrontation or anything that resembles it. The way to handle negativity is to counteract it with the opposite polarity—-positiveness. To remain positive, loving and kind no matter what anyone has done to you is a lofty ideal worth aspiring to. Just trying to do this is enough.

CONCLUSION

∞

We as a species are the only living forms on Earth that can be conscious of ourselves; however, the range of development and awareness within our species is wide and broad. This goes back to the experience we chose this time as we came from Spirit to form on planet Earth. The progression to awareness is contingent on the scope of the experience and the balance of karma we chose this time. To be clear on this…the awareness, the opportunity to be awake and conscious was designed by our Spirit in conjunction with our Source coupled with the karmic balance we desired, chose to explore, be exposed to and live while in form this time. One may ask where choice comes in once we are in form. The choice is always our Response to what happens with the events of our life. The choice directly affects the level of consciousness to which we chose to awaken.

Life is Difficult. It certainly appears to be when we look at the madness existing in the human race, but it doesn't have to be. How can this consciousness of life, being difficult, change and shift? Begin with Gratitude. Begin everyday with Thank You. Stay alert and aware of every blessing occurring moment by moment in your life on this plane. Don't Judge or have any Expectations—Just Do Your Best.

Say Thank You to the beauty of the flower, the birth of a new day, the smile in a child's eyes, the hug a friend gives you. Then when you see and feel the negative, pray in the words of St. Francis, "Make me a Channel of your Peace….." When we pray we need to be detached from the outcome.

Prayer is personal. My morning and evening prayer is, "Glory to God and the power of the Cosmic, I thank you for the blessing of this day, your protection and Love. I ask to be a continued channel of service for the greater good….To God be the Glory." Praying is not begging and bargaining, but an acknowledgment of gratitude and a request from above for assistance in your service, in your life. If the only prayer you ever say is thank you, that is enough. The power of prayer is intention and hopefully our intention is to send Love, Healing and Peace to our fellow humans participating in this journey, this time on planet earth with us.

This manuscript concludes with a passage called "The Spirit Community" written by a Vietnamese Zen teacher Thich Nhat Hanh.

"These days, the sangha (the spiritual community) is the Buddha. Many other people share this view: that the enlightened messiah, who has come to save humanity today, is not a person but a collective awakening.

The most reliable teacher is friends meeting friends. When you find a group of friends who care about the truth, who care about each other, and who share a similar depth of maturity and humor about themselves and each other, you have found your sangha.

Value it deeply; it is the boat that will carry you safely across the swamps of imagined separation."

In Love & In Peace

Thank You

NAMASTE

19741208R00067

Made in the USA
Charleston, SC
09 June 2013